Contents

Wars do not end of themselves, there must be a strategy for making them end.

–Dr. Michael Handel

Introduction

It is as critical for the United States to prepare for war termination in the event of a conflict with China as it is to prepare for the conflict itself. Air-Sea Battle (ASB) proposes concepts for military interaction between the two countries, but fails to specify how military leadership is to set the conditions for a transition from Phase 3 to Phase 0 operations.[1] An armed conflict over the disputed Spratly Islands in the South China Sea (SCS) is not impossible, and such a war could involve a Chinese strike against America's power projection forces and infrastructure in the Pacific. Should that happen, the political leadership will task the Joint Force Commander (JFC) with setting the military conditions required to terminate the conflict in line with the United States' strategic objectives. This paper outlines the war termination plan following a notional attack by China that disables an American aircraft carrier and bombards American bases in Guam and Okinawa, while Chinese amphibious forces simultaneously execute an assault to capture islands in the SCS currently occupied by Vietnam, the Philippines and Malaysia.[2]

Following the Chinese strike, an operational plan should initially advocate coercive diplomacy and avoid escalation to facilitate war termination through a negotiated peace. If this approach fails the JFC can then exploit factor time to ratchet-up military and non-military costs while managing the associated risks of vertical and horizontal escalation.[3] A plan that provides a strategy for denying China's initial aims to control and exploit the islands and then offers options for de-escalation acknowledges the unique aspects of Chinese culture and strategic concerns and may allow the U.S. to achieve its objectives with lower

1

costs and less risk than other military-centric courses of action. The operational plan must

account for political pressure demanding expedient retaliation, but mainland strikes

attempting contested disarmament carried out from the sea or by a penetrating manned

bomber, as advocated by the ASB concept, do not contribute to the strategic objective or the

desired end state. [4]

Background

China sees its rightful place as the East Asian hegemon and seeks to resume the role it

occupied until the end of the Qing dynasty and the age of European colonialism.[5] The

Chinese do not subscribe to the view of the sea as a global commons.[6] Nor do they embrace

mare liberum.[7] Those ideas are Western in nature, first promoted by Dutch lawyer Hugo

Grotius in 1609, and do not reflect Chinese tradition. The Chinese do not view restricting

access to the near seas as denying anything to which any other nation has a legitimate claim.[8]

Peter Dutton, Director of the Chinese Maritime Studies Institute, has said:

> For the U.S., the world's EEZs[9] are critical regions in which naval power must
> be brought to bear in support of two fundamental sources of stability for the global
> system: deterrence of international armed conflict, and suppression of nontraditional
> threats to commerce and other activities. For China, however, its EEZ and other
> jurisdictional waters are zones in which outside interference is an unwelcome
> intrusion into domestic security issues, a zone of competition for resources with
> neighboring states that claim overlapping rights, and a region in which national, not
> international, maritime power should dominate."[10]

Unfortunately for China, the West trespassed in its sphere during the century it fought

civil wars and was subjugated by external powers with different assumptions about access to

the sea.[11] The balance of power in the Western Pacific has also shifted since the last time

China was dominant. Historically, China's neighbors were in no position to contest its

influence whereas today they are more independent and prosperous.[12] Globalization enables

these success stories through increased international trade moving across secure sea lines of

2

communication.[13] The modern West has underwritten global maritime security since the end of World War II and has established a framework for trade, cooperation, and security. This security has allowed the benefits of globalization to reach every nation in the Western Pacific and has helped establish ties between these nations and the Western. Because of this, and until recently, other nations in the region have had the option of choosing their own path towards development and governance independent of Chinese influence. This may change as China reemerges and the competition over resources accelerates. The U.S. seeks to maintain access to the commons and develop economic relationships with any nation willing to adopt western free-market rule-sets for trade.[14] Secretary of State Clinton said "strategically, maintaining peace and security across the Pacific is increasingly crucial to global progress, whether through defending freedom of navigation in the SCS or ensuring transparency in military activities of the key players."[15]

This desire for economic security builds on a national security theory advocated by geostrategic theorists such as Nicholas Spykman and H. J. Mackinder, where the defense of an insular nation (the U.S.) is secured in the rimlands proximate to the continental power of central Asia.[16] Forward basing, presence and the ability to play the "away game" versus defending from the American coast were central tenets of Mahan and reasons for war in 1917 and 1941, and are still critical to securing the nation and the current world order.[17] The value of the object for the U.S. in the Western Pacific has been and will continue to be high, and the Chinese should expect the U.S. to defend tenaciously its forward presence as a pillar of national security.[18]

The strategic prize is the long-term disposition of the Western Pacific: will it conform to an American-led international order or one dominated by an unreconstructed Chinese hegemony?[19] As the Chinese economic miracle unfolds, the once insular state is looking to reoccupy its place as the Middle Kingdom and secure access to the resources found there.[20] Although state-on-state conflict may appear unlikely due to economic interdependence, the deep-rooted differences in ideology and vision for the future of the region may bring powers, great and small, into conflict. After watching China's economic strength return and its military modernize at a faster pace than anyone predicted even 10 years ago,[21] President Obama announced a strategic pivot towards Asia.[22] In 1996, the deployment of two U.S. carriers to the Taiwan Straits embarrassed China and inspired it to develop Anti-Access and Area Denial (A2/AD) systems.[23] These systems are capable of targeting warships within 900 nautical miles of the coast[24] and land targets as far as Guam.[25]

The U.S. has countered with the ASB concept; it is a two part plan designed to defend against an initial barrage of Chinese ballistic and cruise missiles by using active and passive defense, and then destroy Beijing's offensive capability through coordinated strikes on China's command and control and launch platforms on the mainland and at sea. This would enable U.S. forces to operate in areas previously denied by A2/AD. Air-Sea Battle is not designed as a war-winning concept, but rather one that balances China's military power in the region.[26]

Hypothetical Road to War

China may conclude that the benefit of using hostile force to seize the Spratly Islands is worth the risk of a confrontation with the U.S.[27] China nevertheless respects the power projection capability of the U.S. and so, in this fictitious but plausible scenario, has decided to execute an unannounced first strike to blind the American command and control network and prevent the use of forward basing for air assets and naval vessels.[28] Authoritative

Chinese military literature suggests the PLA[29] would conduct large-scale preventative attacks designed to disable U.S. forces based or operating in the Pacific.[30] China's A2/AD aims to push U.S. forces out of range of the mainland and also constrain U.S. operational logistics.[31]

This hypothetical scenario will initially be a war with limited aims using limited means.[32] Neither side entered the conflict with total domination and forced unconditional capitulation as an objective, nor would China have attacked if it thought a retaliatory nuclear strike from the U.S. was likely.[33] The limited objective for the Chinese is the capture of the Spratly Islands[34] and the objective for the U.S. is a return to the status quo *ante bellum*. Barring a change in objectives, this conflict will end through a negotiated peace.[35] It is the responsibility of the JFC to set military conditions that allow the political leadership to exercise options for war termination.[36]

Human Terrain and Recent Interactions with the Chinese

China's history and culture play heavily into their respect for power and the Chinese have difficulty backing down with any potential for loss of face.[37] According to Ambassador Joseph W. Prueher, the chief U.S. negotiator following the 2001 EP-3 incident, negotiating with the Chinese centers on "building ladders for the Chinese to climb down."[38] The Chinese also respect strength. The operational pause in U.N. offensive operations during negotiations in the Korean War, intended as a sign of graciousness, was instead misinterpreted by the Chinese as an indication of weakness.[39] The pause emboldened the Chinese negotiators and prolonged the conflict. The war termination plan, and the negotiators, should account for these cultural differences.[40]

Developing an Operational Plan

The most desirable outcome for war termination is a negotiated peace that is acceptable to each side. A negotiated peace would deliver the fastest return to normalcy and minimize further bloodshed. Achieving a negotiated settlement may not be possible if the Chinese stick to untenably aggressive positions or the American public demands massive strikes in retribution, but should be pursued until it becomes impossible based on further interaction. An escalatory move by either side is likely irreversible and would eliminate termination options for what began as a limited war. Escalation builds a ladder that may be impossible to climb down. This conflict may transition to one with unlimited objectives but does not have to start off that way. In light of this, the JFC should develop an operational plan that makes an attempt for a negotiated peace and then moves on if that proves impossible. The plan has two major stages.

Stage 1

The Stage 1 objective is war termination that results from coercive diplomacy and avoids counterproductive escalation while imposing costs that promote convergence.[41] The center of gravity is the Chinese Communist Party (CCP), and it has a number of non-military critical vulnerabilities which are listed below. This stage will attempt to coerce the leadership of the CCP by indirect methods that either avoid escalation or attempt to limit escalation. Although this portion of the operational plan will go beyond the use of military force and be difficult for the JFC to manage, it provides options to apply pressure with less risk and lower cost than the mainland strike portion of the ASB.

Since this is a war with limited objectives, an escalatory move extends the ladder. The JFC must avoid unintended escalation as the result of poorly conceived military plans that undermine the strategic objective. Dr. Ronald Spiller, a war termination theorist, said, "Every military action should be designed with a view to the contribution it might make

6

along with that of the enemy to the nature of the peace that will inevitably follow and on no other basis."[42] Operational objectives, when achieved, should deny Chinese aims, afford China de-escalatory options, and to threaten constantly increasing costs for failure to comply.[43] Stage 1 objectives include,

Stage 1 Objectives:

- Execute a strategic communication (SC) plan that addresses the CCP, the American people, and the regional governments utilizing public announcements and private communication.
- Deliver a proportionate military response
- Deny Chinese aims, in this case the aims of reclaiming the Spratly Islands, gaining international recognition for possession of those islands, and exploiting resources.
- Execute a cost imposition plan that applies coercive pressure on the Chinese and avoids counterproductive escalation while promoting convergence.

A plan to achieve each of these objectives is detailed below:

Strategic Communication (Stage 1)

The Strategic Communication (SC) plan[44] will be a vital contributor to successful operations and ultimately war termination. The SC plan should target three audiences: the Chinese leadership, the regional governments and the American people.[45] The public message should emphasize American resolve, the U.S. commitment to the region, and the understanding that escalation of the conflict is only counterproductive. Privately, the U.S. should communicate the desire to return to the status quo, that there are many methods of increasing the cost for the Chinese should they refuse these terms, and that the U.S. has the means and will to impose those costs.[46] Allowing the Chinese to preserve some face publicly contributes to the objective, and explaining U.S. intentions privately gives them more room to negotiate.[47] The SC plan will also coordinate diplomatic efforts with military action.

Proportionate Response (Stage 1)

Through power projection and undersea warfare, the U.S. should target Chinese naval vessels in the SCS in a tit-for-tat manner until the Chinese have suffered losses equal to those of the U.S. The U.S. could announce the targeting of the Chinese aircraft carrier, either in port or at sea, as a reprisal for the strike against the American carrier in the initial attack. Limiting the response to the PLAN and its offensive power projection capability reduces the chances for escalation while satisfying the demands of the American people for a proportionate response. These strikes will also serve to deny Chinese aims in the SCS.

Deny Chinese Aims (Stage 1)

The U.S. and the targeted countries do not need to defeat their common adversary on the Chinese mainland. Bruce Bade defines war termination as "the process of deciding when and how to stop fighting when it becomes evident that war fighting objectives have been met or, are no longer achievable" and the U.S can take China's objective of seizing the islands off the table.[48] The U.S. will also have the opportunity to take the moral high ground by demonstrating to the world that China struck first. An information operations plan, coordinated with SC, could support this objective by filming the Chinese actions and documenting the damage they caused. U.S. should then lead an effort, along with the other countries targeted by China, to garner international consensus condemning the attacks and refuse to recognize Chinese claims on the disputed islands and deny the Chinese desire for legitimacy.[49]

Any contest in the SCS will likely present a power-projection challenge for each competitor,[50] though the U.S. has a marked advantage in that department. China's land-based aircraft will be at the limits of their combat effectiveness,[51] and China possesses only a fraction of the ship-based air defense capability that the U.S. operates in 7th Fleet.[52] China will also be forced to deploy and protect an amphibious force and then execute a contested landing on numerous islands. The islands are small, but the current residents have installed

fixed fortifications and sea-based obstacles to complement the natural barriers to landing.[53]

Contested amphibious assaults are notoriously difficult, and anything the U.S. could

contribute to repelling the Chinese attack could tip the scales in favor of the defense.[54] The

JFC could consider airborne or seaborne insertion of defensive land forces or surface-to-air

missile systems. U.S. or allied submarines in the area could target key elements of the

Chinese fleet. Absent amphibious assault ships, the Chinese will not have the tools required

to achieve their aims. Even if China was to execute a successful amphibious operation, the

drilling equipment required to recover resources will be vulnerable to attack from long-range

weapons that the U.S. or another country could use at any time. Undersea exploration and

extraction of oil and natural gas cannot be accomplished in contested waters. Simply

occupying the islands, even in the face of international condemnation, does not let Beijing

achieve its aims.

The U.S. should use ASB's defensive components to preserve the ability to absorb an

initial strike. The ASB idea of defense supports the aim-denial objective by investing in

operational protection, thereby increasing the number of functional systems, platforms, and

bases following an attack.[55] The capability to intercept missiles in flight, combined with the

ability to withstand or quickly repair the damage inflicted by missiles that make it through,

should be expanded. These systems will allow the JFC to execute military response options

to deny aims and impose costs sooner than if the facilities and platforms were destroyed.

Impose costs (Stage 1)

The U.S. can threaten to use its asymmetric advantage in factor time and factor force

to impose ever-increasing military costs on the Chinese. The U.S. possesses a technological and operational advantage in the area of submarine warfare,[56] where the American fleet of modern attack boats can operate in stealth while targeting Chinese naval forces in the deep waters of the SCS.[57] Using these submarines and advantages in ISR,[58] the U.S. could, for example, announce publicly or convey privately that it will sink one Chinese warship at a time until China agrees to international demands for the return of the disputed islands and to stand down its offensive military forces.[59]

If the U.S. communicates its demands in a way the Chinese understand and then demonstrates the willingness and capability to enforce the consequences of failure of compliance with those demands by sinking ships, it can coerce the Chinese leadership by threatening to increase costs while simultaneously providing an avenue for terminating the conflict. The JFC may target ships of lower value first and then threaten the high-end PLAN ships later on as a method of encouraging the Chinese to accept terms. This systematic method of ratcheting-up costs may adequately address the SC targets in China and at home. This part of the operation could be performed in conjunction with the proportionate response, and coordinated with other regional countries affected by Chinese aggression.

China already operates in an unfriendly neighborhood of its own creation, and the capability of neighboring maritime states to restrict Chinese freedom of maneuver is accelerating yearly even without American-sponsored proliferation of weaponry.[60] The technological "piggybacking" that China mastered in decades past has been emulated to great effect by its smaller neighbors, ones who have now closed the weapons capability gap to a narrow margin.[61] As an example, Vietnam will have the ability to perform sea-denial operations out to approximately 300km from its coast or islands in the SCS.[62] The proliferation of quiet submarines, advanced air defenses, and long-range anti-ship cruise missiles launched from shore, aircraft, surface vessels and submarines could create access problems for the Chinese.[63] Overlaying weapons ranges on the first island chain restricts the maneuver space surrounding China. The PLAN risks being hemmed in by weapons similar to or even identical to those Beijing procured to ensure freedom of access for itself.[64] The U.S. could use the prospect of proliferation of these weapons to apply coercive pressure on the Chinese in two different ways: either threaten to promote the proliferation of A2/AD, or offer American influence in bilateral relationships to discourage it. The carrot and the stick are available to the political leadership and should be incorporated into Stage 1.

In this scenario the U.S. has the advantage in factor time.[65] China's missile arsenal does not possess strategic depth,[66] and if the primary volleys are unsuccessful the Chinese do not have a credible fallback option.[67] Missiles are one-use weapons, and if the U.S. weathers the initial strike it can use ships and aircraft to apply continuous pressure on the adversary. By weathering the initial strike, the U.S. can turn factor time into an advantage since China would have expended its most capable weapon and the timings of the counterstrike, and therefore, the initiative is left to the U.S.

Stage 1 can continue until war termination is achieved or the political leadership tells the JFC there is no more time. Stage 2 will occur sequentially if Stage 1 does not result in war termination.

Stage 2

The transition from Stage 1 to Stage 2 will take place when all opportunities for a low-cost negotiated peace have been exhausted, and the desired end state cannot be achieved through strategic restraint and coercive diplomacy.[68] Stage 2 represents a long-term contest between international systems and the U.S. must demonstrate that its vision for the world can

11

survive without Chinese participation and in spite of Chinese aggression. In Stage 2 the operational plan will accept the risk of escalation and transition from efforts to achieve a negotiated peace to directly threatening the regime.

The JFC and civilian leadership will have two options regarding the Chinese communist regime: reconcile with it and offer to negotiate termination while not threatening it from within or without,[69] or failing that attempt to topple it so that negotiations can proceed with different leadership.[70] Michael Vickers, from the SCBA, comments "ending a war with China may mean affecting some form of regime change, because we do not want to leave some wounded, angry regime in place."[71] The JFC should consider how U.S. political leaders might view the value of the object versus the risk of threatening the regime and implement portions of this Stage 2 plan in accordance with their guidance. Stage 2 will,

- Blockade China to inflict economic damage and encourage domestic unrest.[72]
- Encourage horizontal escalation along China's land borders.
- Execute maritime trade warfare, establish and secure SLOCs for trade with all regional allies and keep the international order intact and trade alive in spite of China's efforts to target it.

Targeting Domestic Stability and the Chinese Economy (Stage 2)

Perhaps China's most daunting task over the next few decades will be managing its domestic issues such as demographic imbalances and slowing domestic growth.[73] Even without war with the U.S., China's continued stability is tenuous, and, with foreign powers deliberately attempting to incite domestic unrest in this scenario, the problem only becomes more severe.[74] Actions targeting the Chinese economy, particularly its reliance on imported sources of energy and resources, could apply pressure on the leadership and indirectly threaten its hold on power and control over the population.[75] This could be accomplished through maritime trade warfare.

Maritime Trade Warfare (Stage 2)

Although a blockade may have a negligible effect on China's military capacity due to the central government's ability to restrict domestic consumption, the impact on economic growth and the associated domestic stability concerns may act as a coercive force.[76] Economists claim that a minimum of 8% growth is required to maintain stability and a limited blockade and embargo could cause growth to fall below that threshold.[77] The JFC could enforce this blockade through a number of different mechanisms.[78] Simply stopping all outbound shipments from the U.S. to China will have a tremendous impact, and the participation of other states in the blockade and embargo will magnify the effect.[79] America's factor force advantage would allow it to control key chokepoints around the globe and intercept Chinese-bound shipments beyond the reach of the PLAN. The blockade does not have to be air tight but just effective enough to hurt growth. Offensive maritime trade warfare has the benefit of reversibility, and unless it targets shipping capacity, the punitive effect of the blockade can be turned off immediately. The SLOCs between allies should be secured by defensive maritime warfare. The JFC must also prioritize the return of normal trading patterns between regional partners by defending SLOCs against Chinese threats to trade. These allies may want to take military action as well.

Encouraging Horizontal Escalation (Stage 2)

China does not enjoy any long-term alliances due to a sense of cultural superiority and a lack of common ideology with other states.[80] Of China's 14 land-based neighbors, Pakistan is the only country with which China can claim to have warm ties.[81] Conversely, a number of states have taken a decidedly pro-democratic and anti-Chinese turn in the recent years. Mongolia, India, Pakistan, Bangladesh, Thailand, Vietnam and Malaysia all participate in military exercises with the U. S. and, although the U.S. cannot be assured of their support in a time of crisis, the potential alliance between these countries is troublesome for China.[82] Threats to land borders will force the Chinese leadership, currently straddling the line between the responsibilities of a continental power and a state with aspirations for global power projection, to shift its focus away from the sea. The JFC must develop branch plans that detail options to limit horizontal escalation, or attempt to manage escalation once third parties have entered the conflict of their own accord. If the Chinese have hunkered down and isolated themselves like they did following international condemnation of the Tiananmen Square incident in 1989,[83] the operational plan could have branches that actively encourage horizontal escalation. Each of the steps in Stage 1 and Stage 2 let the JFC set the conditions for the political leadership to terminate the war. None of these recommendations included mainland strikes.

The Operational Utility of the Air-Sea Battle Concept

The ASB article submitted by the Chief of Naval Operations and the Chief of Staff of the Air Force describes three lines of effort: *Disrupt, Destroy, Defeat.*[84] Under *Destroy*, the line of action recommends, "Offensive operations to neutralize adversary weapon delivery platforms such as ships, submarines, aircraft and missile launchers."[85] The ASB plan to develop the capability to fly persistently over mainland China and strike its mobile missile launchers[86] may be unrealistic from a factor force perspective. The SCUD hunting effort in Operation DESERT STORM was more difficult than estimated and ultimately unsuccessful.[87] Even with the benefit of air supremacy and special force spotters on the ground, Iraqi missile launchers were nearly impossible to distinguish from decoys and few, if any, were destroyed by strikes from fixed-wing aircraft.[88] Targeting the weapons, could also

14

be counterproductive due to China's reaction to a strike on the mainland and the escalatory pressure such a strike would apply. The "ladder" the Chinese would have to climb down during negotiations would only get taller, and those strikes are unlikely to ever fully disarm the Chinese. It will be difficult, if not impossible, to guarantee freedom of action in China's near seas by contested disarmament, and efforts to accomplish that may ultimately undermine the desired end state. The U.S. must compel China to allow freedom of navigation within range of the PRC's missiles as a prerequisite for transition to Phase 0.

Conversely, the ASB concept advocates "rolling back" China's strike and ISR capabilities so that the U.S. Navy can operate close enough to Chinese shores to project power inland from aircraft carriers. If there is no need in the operational plan for carrier-based strikes on the mainland then, there will not be a need to defend the carrier close to the Chinese coast.

Counterargument

Some may say that in order to terminate the conflict on favorable terms the JFC must retain enough military capability to operate inside of China's A2/AD bubble. Mainland strikes, as proposed by the ASB concept, represent the only credible military threat to the Chinese and would be vital to achieving the desired end state. Without all the components of the ASB concept, the commander does not have the tools needed to force the adversary into accepting favorable terms. The Department of Defense recognizes this and has established an Air-Sea Battle cell to develop concepts and coordinate efforts between the Air Force and the Navy.[89]

Also, the American people and regional allies will likely demand revenge for an attack that disabled a carrier and struck U.S. territory.[90] Retreating to remain safe from

Chinese weapons plays directly into the adversary's hands, and would be the first of many steps where the Chinese actively displace American power and influence and exert their own. The U.S. would lose credibility regionally and globally if it were to sue for peace following a strike on a carrier. Air-Sea Battle lets the U.S. take the fight to the enemy's doorstep and impose its will using overwhelming military force, and that response is the only one the Chinese will respect.

Rebuttal

The JFC should recognize that the center of gravity is not China's A2/AD capability. China's defenses are focused on protecting the mainland, and the Spratly Islands are far enough away that the strength of the defense begins to dissipate. The Chinese have large numbers of short and medium range missiles, but fewer of the long-range variety required to target distant ships and airbases. Without air-to-air refueling, Chinese fighters will not be able to adequately protect bombers performing strikes in the southern limits of the SCS. It may be possible for the U.S. to achieve the strategic objectives by avoiding military operations in the strength of the Chinese defense. The JFC can develop a plan that will impose costs while remaining at a safer distance.

Escalating the conflict by conducting mainland strikes in futile attempts at contested total disarmament will deny the JFC the operational objectives and put the desired end state further out of reach by making the ladder taller.[91] Even after mainland strikes China will still possess the capability to target aircraft and ships with its weapon systems, and must be compelled not to use those weapons in a return to Phase 0. Strategic communication will be a critical aspect of this conflict, and the American audience deserves particular consideration since advocating an operational plan that does not include an overwhelming response for the loss of life will be difficult. There will likely be pressure for retaliatory strikes, but such strikes may escalate the war and further narrow termination options.[92]

Recommendations

The JFC should develop a plan with an initial stage that slows or prevents escalation while providing the Chinese with cost avoidance incentives for war termination en route to a negotiated peace. If that option is unacceptable for either side, only then should the JFC pursue a second stage that accepts the escalatory risk of threatening the CCP and expanding the war.

Conclusion

The JFC should develop an operational plan with the understanding that any escalatory action against China will likely make the negotiations for war termination more difficult. The ASB concept of destroying mainland A2/AD systems does not address the Chinese center of gravity, and protecting aircraft carriers from missile attack may become a pursuit of diminishing returns.[93] A plan that provides options for de-escalation acknowledges Chinese culture and negotiation style and may allow the U.S. to achieve its strategic objectives with lower costs and less risk than other military-centric courses of action. The U.S. should maintain or develop the capability to deny China its territorial aims in the SCS while applying coercive pressure on China's non-military centers of gravity to encourage convergence and ultimately peace in a western Pacific aligned with the American-led international order.

Notes

[1] Phase 3 of an operation is titled "Dominate" in the joint pub and represents high-end military decisive operation. Phase 0 is labled "Shape" and addresses peacetime activites in a theater. U.S. Office of the Chairman of the Joint Chiefs of Staff. *Joint Operations*. Final Coordination. Joint Publication (JP) 3-0 (Washington DC: CJCS 11 August 2011), III-42.

[2] This scenario is used to examine war termination options in a difficult high-end conflict. If the initial strike is less severe future planners can use parts of this discussion as they apply to another scenario. For an analysis of missile capabilities see: Marshall Hoyler, "China's Antiaccess Ballistic Missiles and U.S. Active Defense," *Naval War College Review* 63, no. 4 (Autumn 2012), 86.

[3] Vertical escalation is an increase in the intensity of conflict between two combatants while horizontal escalation expands the conflict to new areas between the combatants or to previously unengaged parties.

[4] David Axe, "The Air Force accelerates work on a new multi-billion dollar strategic bomber despite the critics," *Wired Magazine*, 26 March 2012, accessed 27 April, 2012, http://www.wired.com/dangerroom/2012/03/airforce-bomber-gamble/ .

[5] David Shambaugh (Professor of Political Science and International Affairs Director, China Policy Program, George Washington University, Lecture at the Naval War College, 11 April 2012).

[6] China is a signatory to the United Nations Convention to the Law on the Seas and ratified the treaty, but disputes Japan's interpretation of UNCLOS II and UNCLOS III in relation to the extension of the Chinese continental shelf and the impact it has on the extent of the Chinese EEZ. Japan's interpretation is in accordance with international law.

[7] Grotius proposed that *mare liberum*, or "The Free Sea" should mean that every country has access to the seas beyond a state's immediate coastline. "Hugo Grotius." *Standford Encyclopedia of Philosoph,.* July 28, 2011, accessed April 10, 2012, http://plato.stanford.edu/entries/grotius/.

[8] Till, Geoffrey. *Seapower: A Guide for the Twenty-First Century Second Edition* (New York: Routledge, 2009). 9

[9] Exclusive Economic Zones as defined by: United Nations General Assembly, "United Nations Convention on the Law of the Sea, Part V" 1983, accessed 27 April 2012.

[10] Peter A. Dutton, "Military Activites in the EEZ: A U.S.-China Dialogue on Secuirty and International Law in the Maratime Commons." *China Maratime Study 7* (Newport, RI: Naval War College, 2010).

[11] Elleman, Bruce A., and S.C.M. Paine. *Modern China* (Upper Saddle River: Prentice Hall, 2010).

[12] South Korea has the world's seventh largest GDP and China just recently overtook Japan for second place behind the U.S. in terms of economic output. The countries to China's south have also prospered with Thailand, Vietnam, Singapore, Malaysia, and Indonesia boasting increased growth; The World Bank, "GDP (current US$)." *The World Bank.* April 22, 2012, accessed April 22, 2012, http://data.worldbank.org/indicator/NY.GDP.MKTP.CD?order=wbapi_data_value_2010+wbapi_data_value+w bapi_data_value-last&sort=desc

[13] Chief of Naval Operations, *A Cooperative Strategy for 21st Century Seapower*, (2007), 4.

[14] Ibid,. 4

[15] Hillary Clinton, "Ameria's Pacific Century." *Foreign Policy* (November 2011).

[16] H. J. Mackinder, "The Geographical Pivot of History" *The Geographical Journal* (Blackwell Publishing on behalf of The Royal Geographical Society) 23, no. 4 (April 1904): 412-437.

[17] Nicholas John Spykman, *The Geography of Peace* (New York: Harcourt, Brace and Company, 1944)

[18] Peter Dutton, (Chinese Maratime Studies Institute, Naval War College, Interview by the author March 2012).

[19] Professor Toshi Yoshihara (U.S. Naval War College Strategy and War Department, Interview by the author March 2012).

[20] Xiaohui (Anne) Wu, "Confucius Could Help Relations Between US, China" *Belfer Center for Science and International Affairs: John F. Kennedy School of Government. Harvard University.* Accessed 3 March 2012, http://belfercenter.ksg harvard.edu/publication/19521/confucius_could_help_relations_between_us_china.html? breadcrumb=%2Fpublication%2F20918%2Fuschina_relationship.

[21] David Shambaugh, "China's Military Modernization: Making Steady and Surprising Progress" *The National Breau of Asian Research*, accessed September 2005, http://www.nbr.org/publications/element.aspx?id=39, 2.

[22] Kenneth Lieberthal, "The American Pivot to Asia" *Foreign Policy* (December 21, 2011).

[23] China was unable to detect or challenge the presense of the U.S. carrier strike groupes. See: Robert S. Ross, "China's Aircraft Carrier: Chinese Naval Nationalism and Its Implications for the United States." *Belfer Center for Science and International Affairs, Harvard Kennedy School.* (October 2011), 13.

[24] The Chinese DF-21D or CSS-5 Mod 5 Anti-ship ballistic missile has an estimated range of 1500 kilometers and is designed to target an aircraft carrier under way at sea. Andrew S Erickson and David D. Yang. "On the Verge of a Game-Changer." *Proceedings* (May 2009), 1,275.

[25] The Chinese could do this by using B-6 bombers carrying air-launched land attack cruise missiles. See: Michael P Flaherty, "Red Wings Ascendant: The Chinese Air Force Contribution to Antiaccess." *Joint Forces Quartely*, (Fall 2011), 95 and Department of Defense. *Annual Report to Congress: Military Power of hte People's Republic of China 2009.* Washington D.C.: Government Printing Office,(2009), 56.

[26] Mark Gunzinger, Andrew F. Krepinevich, Jim Thomas, and Jan van Tol. "AirSea Battle: A Point-of-Departure Operational Concept" *Studies.* (Center for Stragegic and Budgetary Assessments, May 18, 2010).

[27] Ian Storey, "US Concerns in the South China Sea dispute." *The Strait Times*, (April 18, 2012).

[28] Mark Gunzinger, Andrew F. Krepinevich, Jim Thomas, and Jan van Tol. "AirSea Battle: A Point-of-Departure Operational Concept" *Studie,* (Center for Stragegic and Budgetary Assessments, May 18, 2010).

[29] People's Liberation Army

[30] Jixun Yu, "People's Liberation Army Second Artillery Corps." *The Science of Second Artillery Campaigns,* (2004), 401-402.

[31] Mark Gunzinger, Andrew F. Krepinevich, Jim Thomas, and Jan van Tol. "AirSea Battle: A Point-of-Departure Operational Concept" *Studies,* (Center for Stragegic and Budgetary Assessments, May 18, 2010).

[32] This is the Claueswitizian definition of limited war in relation to strategic objectives. "War can be of two kinds, in the sense that either the objective is to overthrow the enemy - to render him politically helpless or militarily impotent, thus forcing him to sign whatever peace we please; or merely to occupy some of his frontier-districts so that we can annex them or use them for bargaining at the peace negotiations" (Carl von Clausewitz, On War, ed and trans. Michael Howard and Peter Paret (Princeton NJ: Princeton University Press 1984), 69.

[33] Assuming China has the limited aim of reclaiming the Spratly Islands, it would not have started this conflict if it though the U.S. would perform mainland nuclear strikes due to a rational cost-benefit analysis. See: Michael Richardson, "China Targeting U.S. Deterrence." *The Japan Times Online.* (January 5, 2011), accessed March 2, 2012, http://www.japantimes.co.jp/text/eo20110105mr.html.

[34] In addition to resources, the Chinese view the Spratly Islands as territory unjustly occupied by other countries, and wish to reclaim them as a point of national pride.

[35] "Most wars end by negotiations between the opposing parties. This is especially the case in wars with limited political strategic objectives." Vego, *Joint Operational Planning: Theory and Practice* (Newport, RI:Naval War College Press, 2007), IX-178.

[36] Fondaw, Jeffrey E. "Conflict Termination--Considerations for the Operational Commander." (Newport, RI: Naval War Collge, May 2001), ii.

[37] The Chinese have also have strategic reasons for not backing down in this scenario which are similar to the concerns of the U.S. But, the importance of saving face is greater in Chinese culture that it is for someone with a Western perspective and the war termination plan and the negotiators should acknowledge and prepare for this.

[38] Bruce Elleman, "The Right Skill Set." in *Ninteen-Gun Salute*, ed. John B. Hattendorf and Burce E. Elleman, (Newport, RI: Naval War College Press, 2009), 242.

[39] General Ridgeway, commander of U.N. forces during negotiations with the Chinese during the Korean War, said "Communists understand only what they want to understand, they consider courtesy as a concession and a concessions as weakness...and that we should employ such language and methods as these treacherous savages cannot fail to understand, and understanding, respect." William Stueck, *Rethinking the Korean War.* (Princeton, NJ: Princeton University Press, 2004), 207.

[40] The operational factor of space encompasses not only the physical environment and weather/climate but also the so-called "human-space." Vego, Milan. *Joint Operational Planning: Theory and Practice,* (Newport, RI: U.S. Naval War College Press, 2007), III-7.

[41] "The convergence of aims is not produced on the battlefield alone. It derives not from only military actions but also from influences well beyond the battlefield, only some of which may be within the reach of control by policymakers, strategists, and operational commanders." Roger Spiller, "War Termination: Theory and

American Practice." *War Termination: Proceedings of the War Termination Conference United States Military Academy West Point.* (Fort Leavenworth, KS: Combat Studies Institute, June 2010), 7-16.

[42] Roger Spiller, "War Termination: Theory and American Practice." *War Termination: Proceedings of the War Termination Conference United States Military Academy West Point.* (Fort Leavenworth, KS: Combat Studies Institute, June 2010). 7-16.

[43] Edward A. Rice, "The Operational Commander and War Termination on Favorable Terms." (Newport, RI: Naval War College, February 3, 1989), 21.

[44] U.S. Office of the Chairman of the Joint Cheifs of Staff. *Joint Operational Planning.* Final Coordination. Joint Publication (JP) 5-0 Annex Y (Washington DC: CJCS 11 August 2011), A-9.

[45] The JFC will not have sole responsibility for developing the SC strategy. The Secretary of Defense Memo from 25 January 2011 regarding SC and IO states "The Under Secretary of Defense for Policy (USD(P)) and the Assistant Secretary of Defense for Public Affairs (ASD(PA)) are formally designated as SC co-leads. Robert Gates. "Memorandum for the Secretaries of the Military Departments: Strategic Communication and Information Operations in the DoD." (January 25, 2011).

[46] A possible message may read: *The United States condemns the unprovoked attack on our armed forces and on the other countries with territory in the South China Sea. Our objective is a return to the status quo and we will act to prevent the exchange of territory through the use of force. We also demand that China recognize the rights to freedom of navigation in accordance with UNCLOS. We will not abandon the region. We will not target the Chinese mainland with punitive strikes, but will destroy offensive sea-based weapon systems until China agrees to these terms. If China does not accept these terms, we will lead an international effort to restore territory lost to the Chinese and will actively target the communist regime.*

[47] Chinese nationalism should be considered in any SC plan, and the operational plan should have objectives that support the strategic level. The CCP will probably use Chinese nationalism as a tool to secure power and the support of the people, and JFC must consider how any action targeting China will affect the relationship between the people and the leadership conducting negotiations. "We often think of nationalism as a reactionary sentiment, a relic of the 19th century. Yet it is traditional nationalism that mainly drives politics in Asia, and will continue to do so. That nationalism is leading unapologetically to the growth of militaries in the region -- navies and air forces especially -- to defend sovereignty and make claims for disputed natural resources. There is no philosophical allure here. It is all about the cold logic of the balance of power. To the degree that unsentimental realism, which is allied with nationalism, has a geographical home, it is the South China Sea." Robert Kaplan, "The South China Sea is the Future of Conflict The 21st century's defining battleground is going to be on water, *Foreign Policy,* (September/October 2011).

[48] Bruce Bade, C. *War Termination: Why Don't We Plan For It in Essays on Strategy XII.* ed by John N. Petrie. (Washington D.C: National Defense University Press, 1994).

[49] Currently the U.S. position regarding the Spratly Islands is non-partisan, but during the negotiation the U.S. could threaten to internationalize the issue and propose arbitration of the disputes over the islands. The U.S. could also recognize the claims of Vietnam, Malaysia, and the Philipines and state that China's claims are not valid. This approach may apply coercive pressure on the Chinese while avoiding escalation and keeping the "ladder" short.

[50] The Spratly Islands are between 650 and 900 nautical miles away from the closest Chinese People's Liberation Army Navy (PLAN) or People's Liberation Army Air Force (PLANAF) bases on mainland China. There are Chinese PLAN and PLANAF bases on Hainan Island and in the Paracel Islands (seized from Vietnam in 1971), which are approximately 100 and 300 nautical miles closer respectively.

[51] China does not have an operational air-to-air refueling capability to extend the range or on-station time of its tactical aircraft. Department of Defense, *Annual Report to Congress: Military Power of the People's Republic of China 2009* (Washington D.C.: Government Printing Office, 2009), 56.

[52] *The Economist.* "The Dragon's New Teeth." (April 7, 2012), 35-39.

[53] Cynthia D. Balana, "Philippines behind other Spratlys claimants in building defensive structures." *Phillipine Daily Inquirer*, (June 16, 2011).

[54] "A landing on a foreign coast in the face of hostile troops has always been one of the most difficult operations of war." -Captain Sir Basil H. Liddell Hart.

[55] Jim Garamone, "Pentagon Office to Coordinate New Air-Sea Strategy." *U.S. Department of Defense: Armed Forces Press Service.* (November 10, 2011). http://www.defense.gov/news/newsarticle.aspx?id=66042 (accessed March 4, 2012).

[56] Owen R Cote,. "Assessing the Undersea Balance Between the U.S. and China." *MIT Security Studies Program Working Group.* (Feb 2011), accessed April 24, 2012, http://web.mit.edu/ssp/publications/working_papers/Undersea%20Balance%20WP11-1.pdf .

[57] The Pentagon plan also calls for expanded investment in the Virginia-class attack submarines. Halloran, Richard. "AirSea Battle." *Air Force Magazine*, (August 2010), 44-48.

[58] Intellignece, Surveilence and Reconnance See: O'Rourke, Ronald. *China Naval Modernization: Implications for U.S. Navy Capabilites-Background and Issues for Congress.* (Washington D.C.: Congressional Research Service, 2012), 40.

[59] "This indirectly supports the bargaining process by impressing on the opponent the need to end the hostilities quickly rather than waiting and suffering more losses. Milan Vego, *Joint Operational Planning: Theory and Practice* (Newport, RI: Naval War College Press 2007), IX-180.

[60] Joseph S. Nye. "U.S.-China Relationship: A Shift in Perceptions of Power." *Belfer Center Programs or Projects: International Security.* (April 6, 2011). http://belfercenter.ksg harvard.edu/publication/20918/uschina_relationship.html (accessed March 2, 2012).

[61] Leithen Francis. "Unsettled Waters: Southeast Asian nations buld up air defenses in response to tension in the South China Sea." *Aviation Week and Space Technology*, (March 26, 2012), 67-68.

[62] Jay Menon, "Flexing Muscles: Indai and Pakistan, unasy neighbors, grow their arsenals." *Aviation Week and Space Technology*, (March 26, 2012), 69.

[63] Maj Huy Nguyen, Vietnam People's Army, (interview by the author April 2012).

[64] Geoff Dyer, "China and US create less pacific ocean." *Finicial Times*. (February 12, 2012). http://www.ft.com/intl/cms/s/0/0fdb73c6-53e0-11e1-9eac-00144feabdc0.html#axzz1od12aP8X.

[65] Milan Vego, *Joint Operational Planning: Theory and Practice.* (Newport, RI: U.S. Naval War College, 2007). III-19-38.

[66] Richard N Rosecrance,. "Improving U.S.-China Relations: The Next Steps." *Belfer Center for Science and International Affairs, Harvard Kennedy School.* (August 2009). http://belfercenter.ksg harvard.edu/publication/19513/improving_uschina_relations.html.

[67] Harry Kazianis, "China's Anti-Access Missile." *The Diplomat.* (November 18, 2011). http://the-diplomat.com/flashpoints-blog/2011/11/18/chinaa-anti-access-missile/ (accessed March 4, 2012).

[68] Sparta did not win the Peloponnesian War by offering a generous peace. They won the war by building a force that targeted the enemies' strength (the Athenian navy) and by the Persian intervention on their behalf.

[69] Jeffrey E. Fondaw, "Conflict Termination--Considerations for the Operational Commander." (Newport, RI: Naval War College, May 2001), 6.

[70] It may be difficult during the war to know if coercive Phase 1 actions are influencing the regime. The provision in the SC plan for private negotiations may provide this information, in addition to human intelligence sources with knowledge of the CCP.

[71] Robert D. Kaplan,. "How We Would Fight China." *The Atlantic*, (June 2005).

[72] David Shambaugh, (lecture at the Naval War College, 11 April 2012).

[73] Joseph S. Nye. "U.S.-China Relationship: A Shift in Perceptions of Power." *Belfer Center Programs or Projects: International Security.* (April 6, 2011). http://belfercenter.ksg harvard.edu/publication/20918/uschina_relationship html (accessed March 2, 2012).

[74] Beijing, for example, sees basically hostile American efforts in the following spheres: promoting dissent in China in order to create instability that America can then fan via cyber activities into upheaval that will bring down the Chinese Communist Party's rule. Lieberthal, Kenneth. "The American Pivot to Asia." *Foreign Policy*, (December 21, 2011).

[75] Henry A. Kissinger,. "The Future of U.S.-Chinese Relations." *Foreign Affairs*, (Apr/May 2012).

[76] William S. Murray and Gabriel S. Collins. "No Oil for the Lamps of China?" *Naval War College Review, Spring 2008, Vol. 61, No. 2*, (Spring 2008), 79-95.

[77] *The Economist. "Reflating the Dragon"* (Novenber 18, 2008).

[78] "Combatant commanders, their staffs, and senior civilian leaders should also bear in mind the need to conduct maritime trade warfare with *all means of national power*, including non-military means when possible. Examples include cyber attacks against the maritime information system of the hostile power, economic and legal trade pressure on ocean carriers, sabotage, diplomatic efforts to curtail third party trade with an enemy, banking and financial restriction against hostile regimes, reductions in foreign aid, and the fomenting of labor unrest and strikes that impact an enemy's ability to conduct maritime commerce. William G. McDonald, *Maritime Trade Warfare: Attack and Defense in the Global Commons,* (Newport: RI, January 2012), 9.

[79] The JFC can propose an embargo to support military objectives, but it will be up to the civilian leaders to balance strategic objectives against the economic cost such an embargo would have in the U.S.

[80] Minxin Pei, "The Loneliest Superpower." *Foreign Policy*, (March 20, 2012).

[81] Kamran Yousaf, "Joint military exercise: Pakistan, China begin war games near Jhelum." *Internatinoal Herald Tribune, Pakistan*, (November 15, 2011).

[82] Kenneth Lieberthal, "The American Pivot to Asia." *Foreign Policy*, (December 21, 2011).

[83] James Miles, *The legacy of Tinanmen: China in Disarray,* (Unitversity of Michigan Press, 1997), 27-30.

[84] General Norton A. Schwartz, USAF, and Admiral Jonathan W. Greenert, USN. "Air-Sea Battle Promoting Stability in an Era of Uncertainty." *The American Interest.* (February 20, 2012). http://www.the-american-interest.com/article.cfm?piece=1212 (accessed February 27, 2012).

[85] Ibid.

[86] The ASB concept proposes the development of Air Force long-range penetrating strike operations to destroy PLA ground-based long-range maritime surveillance systems and long-range ballistic missile launchers (both anti-ship and land-attack) to expand the Navy's freedom of maneuver and reduce strikes on U.S. and allied bases and facilities.   Mark Gunzinger, Andrew F. Krepinevich, Jim Thomas, and Jan van Tol. "AirSea Battle: A Point-of-Departure Operational Concept." *Studie,* (Center for Stragegic and Budgetary Assessments, May 18, 2010), 5.

[87] Because of failures in intelligence there was "no accurate accounting of numbers of mobile launchers or where they were based [or] hiding. Rear Admiral J. McConnell, interview by Diane T. Putney, Center for Air Force History, and Ronald H. Cole, (JCS Historical Division, February 14, 1992), Quoted in Williamson Murray, *Air War*, (Nautical & Aviation Pub Co of America. July 1995), 166.

[88] Thomas A Keaney, and Eliot A. Cohen. *Gulf War Air Power Survey Report.* (Washington D.C.: Library of Congress, 1993).

[89] General Norton A. Schwartz, USAF, and Admiral Jonathan W. Greenert, USN. "Air-Sea Battle Promoting Stability in an Era of Uncertainty." *The American Interest.* (February 20, 2012). http://www.the-american-interest.com/article.cfm?piece=1212.

[90] Some research suggests the Chinese are developing warheads that will only disable an aircraft carrier and not sink it in order to avoid excessive loss of life. If a single carrie were to sink with all hand (5,300+) then this attack could be more deadly than Pearl Harbor and 9/11 combined. Andrew S. Erickson and David D. Yang. "On the Verge of a Game-Changer." Proceedings (May 2009), 1,275.

[91] The Chinese fear of territorial or sovereign encroachment would be realized by American-led mainland strikes, and such strikes may risk rapid vertical escalation after which the JFC cannot adequately achieve the operational objectives or offer the political leadership choices for war termination. China viewed 1999's Operation ALLIED FORCE in Kosovo as a replay of the Boxer Rebellion of 1898, where an alliance of western powers intervened to exploit a weaker state. As a result China is keenly suspicious of any attempts to impose western rule sets in the region or impinge on their sovereignty. Threatening this is one option for the commander, but is risky and unlikely to contribute to the desired end state.

[92] Fred Charles Ikle, *Every War Must End,* (New York , Columbia University Press 1991), 41-42.

[93] Robert D. Kaplan,. "How We Would Fight China." *The Atlantic*, (June 2005).

Bibliography

Axe, David. "The Air Force accelerates work on a new multi-billion dollar strategic bomber despite the critics." *Wired Magazine*, March 26, 2012.

Bade, Bruce C. *War Termination: Why Don't We Plan For It in Essays on Strategy XII.* Edited by John N. Petrie. Washington D.C: National Defense University Press, 1994.

Balana, Cynthia D. "Philippines behind other Spratlys claimants in building defensive structures." *Phillipine Daily Inquirer*, June 16, 2011.

BBC Vietnam. "Vietnam Received Second Bastion Coastal Defence System." *BBC Vietnam.* October 19, 2011. http://www.bbc.co.uk/vietnamese/vietnam/2011/10/111019_russia_missiles.shtml (accessed April 22, 2012).

Beckley, Michael. "Don't Worry, America: China is Rising But Not Catching Up." *Christian Science Monitor*, December 14, 2011.

—. "To Stay Ahead of China, Stay Engaged in Asia." *Belfer Center for Science and International Affairs, Harvard Kennedy School.* January 2012. Belfer Center for Science and International Affairs, Harvard Kennedy School (accessed March 3, 2012).

Bradshaw, Arthur L. "United States and Mongolia Conduct Exercise Gobi Wolf." *Center for Strategic Leadership* 5-09 (2009).

Burma News Internationa,l "Bangladesh, US begin naval exercise.". September 19, 2011. http://bnionline.net/index.php/news/kaladan/11701-bangladesh-us-begin-naval-exercise.html (accessed April 19, 2012).

Carreno, Jose, Thomas Culora, U.S. Navy (Retired) Captain George Galdorisi, and Thomas Hone. "What's New About the AirSea Battle Concept?" *Proceedings Magazine*, August 2010: 1,290.

Carter, Ashston B., and William J. Perry. *Preventive Defense: A New Security Strategy for America.* Washington, D.C.: Brookings Institute Press, 1999.

Chase, Michael. "The Dragon's Dilemma: A Closer Look at China's Defense Budget and Priorities." *Progressive Policy Institute.* March 4, 2010. http://progressivepolicy.org/the-dragon's-dilemma-a-closer-look-at-china's-defense-budget-and-priorities (accessed March 2, 2012).

Chief of Naval Operatoions, *A Cooperative Strategy for 21st Century Seapower.* United States Navy, 2007.

Clinton, Hillary. "Ameria's Pacific Century." *Foreign Policy*, November 2011.

Commission, U.S.-China Economic and Security Review. *2011 Report to Congress: U.S.-China Economic and Security Review Commission.* One Hundred Twelfth Congress, Washington D.C.: U.S. Government Printing Office, 2011.

Cote, Owen R. "Assessing the Undersea Balance Between the U.S. and China." *MIT Security Studies Program Working Group.* Feb 2011. http://web.mit.edu/ssp/publications/working_papers/Undersea%20Balance%20WP11-1.pdf (accessed April 24, 2012).

Department of Defense. *Annual Report to Congress: Military Power of the People's Republic of China 2009.* Washington D.C.: Government Printing Office, 2009.

Dutton, Peter A. "Military Activites in the EEZ: A U.S.-China Dialogue on Secuirty and International Law in the Maratime Commons." *China Maratime Study 7.* Naval War College, 2010.

Dyer, Geoff. "China and US create less pacific ocean." *Finicial Times.* February 12, 2012. http://www.ft.com/intl/cms/s/0/0fdb73c6-53e0-11e1-9eac-00144feabdc0.html#axzz1od12aP8X (accessed March 9, 2012).

Elleman, Bruce A., and S.C.M. Paine. *Modern China.* Upper Saddle River: Prentice Hall, 2010.

Elleman, Bruce. "The Right Skill Set." In *Ninteen-Gun Salute*, by Hattendorf John B and Burce E. Elleman, 231-243. Newport, RI: Naval War College Press, 2009.

Erickson, Andrew S., and David D. Yang. "On the Verge of a Game-Changer." *Proceedings*, May 2009: 1275.

Flaherty, Michael P. "Red Wings Ascendant: The Chinese Air Force Contribution to Antiaccess." *Joint Forces Quartely*, 2011: 95-101.

Fondaw, Jeffrey E. "Conflict Termination--Considerations for the Operational Commander." May 2001.

Foot, Rosemary. "Chinese Strategies in a US-Hegemonic Global Order: Accommodating and Hedging." *Belfer Center for Science and International Affairs: John F. Kennedy School of Government. Harvard University.* January 2006. http://belfercenter.ksg.harvard.edu/publication/731/chinese_strategies_in_a_ushegem onic_global_order.html?breadcrumb=%2Fpublication%2F20918%2Fuschina_relation ship (accessed March 3, 2012).

—. *Modes of Regional Conflict Management: Comparing Security Cooperation in the Korean Peninsula, China-Taiwan, and the South China Sea.* Cambridge, MA: The MIT Press, 2007.

Foundation, Heritage. "Defending Defense: China's Military Build-up: Implications for U.S. Defense Spending." *The Foreign Policy Initiative.* March 7, 2011. http://www.foreignpolicyi.org/content/defending-defense-chinas-military-build-implications-us-defense-spending (accessed March 2 2012).

Francis, Leithen. "Unsettled Waters: Southeast Asian nations buld up air defenses in response to tension in the South China Sea." *Aviation Week and Space Technology*, March 26, 2012: 67-68.

Friedberg, Aaron L. "The Future of U.S.-China Relations: Is Conflict Inevitable?" *International Security* 30, no. 2 (Fall 2005): 7-45.

Friedman, George. *The Next 100 Years.* Anchor, 2010.

Fulghum, David, and Bill Sweetman. "Strategy Hiccups: Shortages and new threats rattle U.S.'s Asia-Pacific plans." *AviationWeek & Space Technology*, March 5, 2012: 29-30.

Garamone, Jim. "Pentagon Office to Coordinate New Air-Sea Strategy." *U.S. Department of Defense: Armed Forces Press Service.* November 10, 2011. http://www.defense.gov/news/newsarticle.aspx?id=66042 (accessed March 4, 2012).

Gates, Robert. "Memorandum for the Secretaries of the Military Departments: Strategic Communication and Information Operations in the DoD." January 25, 2011.

General Norton A. Schwartz, USAF, and USN, Jonathan W. Admiral Greenert. "Air-Sea Battle Promoting Stability in an Era of Uncertainty." *The American Interest.* February

20, 2012. http://www.the-american-interest.com/article.cfm?piece=1212 (accessed February 27, 2012).

Glain, Stephen. "The Pentagon's New China War Plan." *Salon.* August 13, 2011. http://www.salon.com/2011/08/13/sino_us_stephen_glain/ (accessed March 3, 2012).

Gunzinger, Mark, Andrew F. Krepinevich, Jim Thomas, and Jan van Tol. "AirSea Battle: A Point-of-Departure Operational Concept." *Studies.* Center for Stragegic and Budgetary Assessments, May 18, 2010.

Halloran, Richard. "AirSea Battle." *Air Force Magazine*, August 2010: 44-48.

Hayden, Tom. "America's New Cold War With China." *The Huffington Post.* November 11, 2011. http://www.huffingtonpost.com/tom-hayden/america-china-foreign-policy_b_1100748.html (accessed March 3, 2012).

Hoyler, Marshall. "CHINA'S "ANTIACCESS" BALLISTIC MISSILES AND U.S. ACTIVE DEFENSE ." *Naval War College Review* 63, no. 4 (Autumn 2012).

Hungtington, Samuel P. *The Clash of Civilizations and the Remaking of World Order.* New York, NY: Touchstone, 1997.

Ikle, Fred Charles. *Every War Must End.* New York: Columbia University Press, 1991.

Information Office of the State Council of the People's Republic of China. "What China's Peaceful Development Means to the Rest of the World." *White Papers of the Government.* September 6, 2011. http://www.china.org.cn/government/whitepaper/2011-09/06/content_23362811.htm (accessed March 4, 2012).

Johnson-Freese, Joan, and Tom Nichols. "US Less Dominant But So What." *DoD Buzz.* November 25, 2009. http://www.dodbuzz.com/2009/11/25/us-less-dominant-but-so-what/.

Kaplan, Robert D. "The South China Sea is the Future of Conflict The 21st century's defining battleground is going to be on water." *Foreign Policy*, September/October 2011.

—. "How We Would Fight China." *The Atlantic*, June 2005.

Kazianis, Harry. "China's Anti-Access Missile." *The Diplomat.* November 18, 2011. http://the-diplomat.com/flashpoints-blog/2011/11/18/chinaa-anti-access-missile/ (accessed March 4, 2012).

Keaney, Thomas A., and Eliot A. Cohen. *Gulf War Air Power Survey Report.* Washington D.C.: Library of Congress, 1993.

Kissinger, Henry A. "The Future of U.S.-Chinese Relations." *Foreign Affairs*, Apr/May 2012.

Krepinevich, Andrew F. "Why AirSea Battle?" *Center for Strategic and Budgetary Assessments.* February 2010, 2010. http://www.csbaonline.org/publications/2010/02/why-airsea-battle/ (accessed March 2, 2012).

Layne, Christopher. "The Waning of U.S. Hegemony—Myth or Reality? A Review Essay." *International Security* 34, no. 1 (Summer 2009): 147-172.

Leiby, Michele Langevine. "U.S. assistance to Pakistan buys little goodwill." *The Washington Post*, Apri 17, 2012.

Lieberthal, Kenneth. "The American Pivot to Asia." *Foreign Policy*, December 21, 2011.

Mackinder, H. J. "The Geographical Pivot of History." *The Geographical Journal* (Blackwell Publishing on behalf of The Royal Geographical Society) 23, no. 4 (April 1904): 412-437.

McDonald, William G. *Maratime Trade Warfare: Attack and Defense in the Global Commons.* Joint Maratime Operations, U.S. Naval War College, Naval War College, 2012, 9.

Menon, Jay. "Flexing Muscles: Indai and Pakistan, unasy neighbors, grow their arsenals." *Aviation Week and Space Technology*, March 26, 2012: 69.

Miles, James. *The Legacy of Tinanmen: China in Disarray.* 27-30 vols. University of Michigan Press, 1997.

Murray, William S., and Gabriel S. Collins. "No Oil for the Lamps of China?" *Naval War College Review, Spring 2008, Vol. 61, No. 2*, Spring 2008: 79-95.

Murray, Williamson. *Air War.* Amer: Nautical & Aviation Pub Company of Anerica, 1995.

Nichols, Tom. "Rumors of U.S. Decline are Greatly Exaggerated." *The Toronto Star.* January 2, 2011. http://www.thestar.com/opinion/editorialopinion/article/914307--rumours-of-u-s-decline-are-greatly-exaggerated (accessed March 3, 2012).

Nye, Joseph S. "U.S.-China Relationship: A Shift in Perceptions of Power." *Belfer Center Programs or Projects: International Security.* April 6, 2011. http://belfercenter.ksg.harvard.edu/publication/20918/uschina_relationship.html (accessed March 2, 2012).

O'Rourke, Ronald. *China Naval Modernization: Implications for U.S. Navy Capabilites-Background and Issues for Congress.* Washington D.C.: Congressional Research Service, 2012.

Pei, Minxin. "The Loneliest Superpower." *Foreign Policy*, March 20, 2012.

Pham, Nga. "Vietnam orders submarines and warplanes from Russia." *BBC News.* December 6, 2009. http://news.bbc.co.uk/2/hi/asia-pacific/8415380.stm (accessed April 22, 2012).

Rice, Edward A. "The Operational Commander and War Termination on Favorable Terms." Newport, RI: Naval War College, February 3, 1989.

Richardson, Michael. "China Targeting U.S. Deterrence." *The Japan Times Online.* January 5, 2011. http://www.japantimes.co.jp/text/eo20110105mr.html (accessed March 2, 2012).

Rosecrance, Richard N. "Improving U.S.-China Relations: The Next Steps." *Belfer Center for Science and International Affairs, Harvard Kennedy School.* August 2009. http://belfercenter.ksg.harvard.edu/publication/19513/improving_uschina_relations.html (accessed March 2, 2012).

Ross, Robert S. "China's Aircraft Carrier: Chinese Naval Nationalism and Its Implications for the United States." *Belfer Center for Science and International Affairs, Harvard Kennedy School.* October 2011. http://belfercenter.ksg.harvard.edu/publication/21444/chinas_aircraft_carrier.html?breadcrumb=%2Fpublication%2F20918%2Fuschina_relationship (accessed March 3, 2012).

—. "The 1995-1996 Taiwan Strait Confrontation: Coercion, Credibility, and Use of Force." *International Security*, Fall 2000: 87-123.

Shambaugh, David. "China's Military Modernization: Making Steady and Surprising Progress." *The National Breau of Asian Research.* September 2005. http://www.nbr.org/publications/element.aspx?id=39 (accessed April 21, 2012).

Spiller, Roger. "War Termination: Theory and American Practice." *War Termination: Proceedings of the War Termination Conference United States Military Academy West Point.* Fort Leavenworth, KS: Combat Studies Institute, June 2010. 7-16.

Spykman, Nicholas John. *The Geography of Peace.* New York: Harcourt, Brace and Company, 1944.

Standford Encyclopedia of Philosophy. "Hugo Grotius." July 28, 2011. http://plato.stanford.edu/entries/grotius/ (accessed April 10, 2012).

Storey, Ian. "US Concerns in the South China Sea dispute." *The Strait Times*, April 18, 2012.

Stueck, William. *Rethinking the Korean War.* Princeton, NJ: Princeton University Press, 2004.

Summers, Matt. "PACOM Headlines." *U.S., Malaysia Air Forces Conclude Exercise Cope Taufan 2012.* April 13, 2012. http://www.pacom.mil/web/Site_Pages/Media/News_2012/04/17-US_malaysia-af-conclude-exercise-cope-taufan12.shtml (accessed April 19, 2012).

The Economist. "Reflating the Dragon." Novenber 13, 2008.

The Economist. "The Dragon's New Teeth." April 7, 2012: 35-39.

The Hindu. "Naval exercise with U.S." April 6, 2012.

The Santos Republic. "Thailand to host US-led military exercise." February 7, 2012.

The World Bank. "GDP (current US$)." *The World Bank.* April 22, 2012. http://data.worldbank.org/indicator/NY.GDP.MKTP.CD?order=wbapi_data_value_2010+wbapi_data_value+wbapi_data_value-last&sort=desc (accessed April 22, 2012).

Thucydides. *The History of the Peloponnesian War.* Edited by Robert B Strassler. New York, NY: Simon and Schuster, n.d.

Till, Geoffrey. *Seapower: A Guide forhte Twenty-First Century Second Edition.* New York: Routledge, 2009.

Torode, Greg. "Vietnam, U.S. to hold naval exercises." *South China Morning Post.* June 13, 2011. http://www.viet-studies.info/kinhte/Viet_Naval_excercise_SCMP.htm (accessed April 19, 2012).

U.S. Office of the Chairman of the Joint Cheifs of Staff. "JOINT PUB 5-0: Joint Operation Planning." 2011.

U.S. Office of the Chairman of the Joint Chiefs of Staff. *Joint Operations.* Washington DC: CJCS, 11 August 2011.

United Nations. "United Nations Convention on the Law of the Sea." United Nations, n.d.

Vego, Milan. *Joint Operational Planning: Theory and Practice.* Newport, RI: U.S. Naval War College, 2007.

—. *Major Naval Operations.* Newport, RI: Naval War College Press, 2008.

"Vietnam Builds Naval Muscle." *Asian Times.* March 29, 2012. http://www.atimes.com/atimes/Southeast_Asia/NC29Ae01.html (accessed April 5, 2012).

Whiteneck, Daniel, Michael Price, Neil Jenkins, and Peter Swartz. *The Navy at a Tipping Point: Maritime.* Center for Naval Analysis, 2010.

Willard, Robert F. "Statment Before the Senate Armed Services Committee on U.S. Pacific Command Posture." Feb 28, 2012.

Wu, Xiaohui (Anne). "Confucius Could Help Relations Between US, China." *Belfer Center for Science and International Affairs: John F. Kennedy School of Government. Harvard University.* n.d. http://belfercenter.ksg.harvard.edu/publication/19521/confucius_could_help_relations _between_us_china.html?breadcrumb=%2Fpublication%2F20918%2Fuschina_relati onship.

Yousaf, Kamran. "Joint military exercise: Pakistan, China begin war games near Jhelum." *Internatinoal Herald Tribune, Pakistan*, November 15, 2011.

Yu, Jixun. "People's Liberation Army Second Artillery Corps." *The Science of Second Artillery Campaigns*, 2004: 401-402.

www.ingramcontent.com/pod-product-compliance
Lightning Source LLC
Chambersburg PA
CBHW081809280526
45789CB00008B/3060